Written by Karen Ferry

Illustrated by Selinah Bull

BENSON THE BOXER

A STORY OF LOSS AND LIFE

Written by Karen Ferry

Illustrated by Selinah Bull

Printed in Australia

For information about permission to reproduce selections from this book, write to:
Permissions, Brain Smart Enterprises Pty Ltd, PO Box 242, Upper Beaconsfield, VIC. 3808

Neuropsychotherapy advisor - Pieter Rossouw

Production manager and editor – Jonathan Wills

Cover artwork - Selinah Bull: selinah@selinahbull.com
Photography of artwork - Aaron Bellette: aibphotography@gmail.com
Design layout - Cameron Ferry: cameron@nyidedesign.com

Title: Benson the Boxer: A Story Of Loss And Life

ISBN – 978-0-6483275-0-9

1. Neuropsychotherapy. 2. Psychotherapy. 3. Brain-based therapy.
4. Neuroscience. 5. Brain Research. 6. Childrens books. 7. Workbook. 8. Treatment Manual.

Brain Smart Enterprises Pty Ltd t/as CORTXION, PO Box 242, Upper Beaconsfield, VIC. 3808

DEDICATION

This book is dedicated to Joshua and Cameron in memory of their boxer dog Benson. It is also dedicated to every child who has ever experienced a situation of trauma and loss, with the hope that there can be healing and a moving forward from the pain they have experienced.

If you have ever been really frightened or really sad over something that has happened to you, or something that has happened to someone you know, then this book is written just for you!

- It will help to explain why you feel the way you do
- It will also give you ideas so that you don't feel so bad anymore
- And the best part is, it will help you if you are feeling scared now, or again in the future.

Benson was a bouncy, bubbly boxer dog. Some might say he was also just a little bit boisterous, especially if he became super excited!

Benson loved playing outside with his best friend Lucy Labrador. Together they would run through the tall grassy fields, rolling and romping, bouncing and tumbling, simply enjoying the summer sunshine.

The summer rains often filled the dams and waterholes.
Benson and Lucy splashed and played in the muddy
puddles. They barked and laughed as the mud turned
their coats the colour of chocolate.

They played under the garden sprinkler, jumping high above the sparkling droplets, letting the water wash them clean after having fun in the muddy puddles.

Often Benson and Lucy would wander over to the next door farm and chat with the strange and friendly farmyard animals.

Benson and Lucy also loved to explore. They chased each other and played 'hide and seek'. Lucy hid under bushes, but Benson would always try to climb the big old tree at the edge of the garden.
"Silly Billy Benson," laughed Lucy, "dogs don't climb trees!"

But the best time of all was when they played with Lucy's ball. The ball bounced and they jumped! The ball rolled and they ran!

Lucy was so clever she could even catch more than one ball in her mouth at a time. Benson laughed – she really did look quite funny.

One day Benson and Lucy were playing in the park. They were jumping and catching Lucy's favourite red ball.

Benson caught the ball in mid-air and threw it back to Lucy. But instead of the ball reaching Lucy,

it rebounded off a large tree trunk, bounced across the park, zipped between the trees,

and whooshed over the recently mown grass. The ball kept rolling and bouncing, bouncing and rolling until...

it finally rolled onto the nearby road.

Without a moment's hesitation, Lucy gave chase.

She ran after the ball and followed it across the park, between the trees,

over the recently mown grass and straight towards the nearby road!

The faster the ball went, the faster she ran! Faster, faster and still faster she ran!

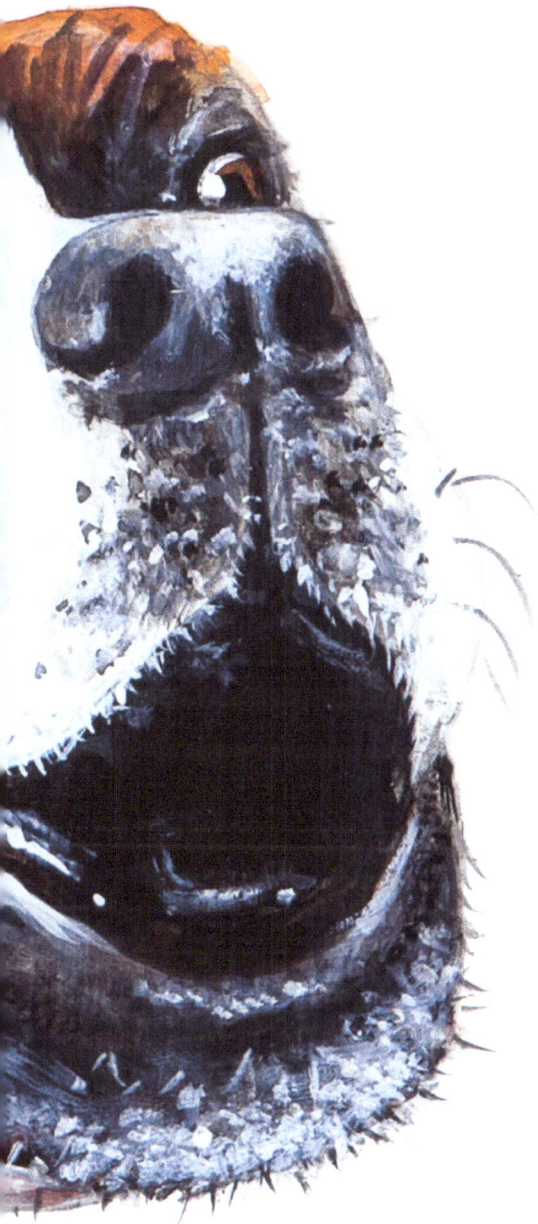

"Oh no," Benson suddenly thought. "This is not good, this looks dangerous!"

He barked and **barked** and **barked**, straining every part of his body, trying to tell his friend Lucy to STOP!!!!!

But Lucy didn't stop. She was running so fast she couldn't hear Benson and she didn't see the danger of the road in front of her.

Feeling scared and desperate, Benson chased after her, frantically trying to catch her before she reached the busy road.

"LUCY! LUCY!!" Benson gave a long and despairing bark,   "**LUCY, STOP!**"

The driver braked hard, but he couldn't stop…

Benson heard a long screech of brakes, he felt a whoosh of wind, then BANG!

Benson stared in horror!

NO! Noooo! He let out a long and sorrowful howl.

Lucy had been hit.
Lucy was dead.

Benson sat stunned.
His heart hurt so badly.

He felt frozen in time and totally numb.

It was a sad day for Benson when he said goodbye to his special friend Lucy. All the animals gathered at Lucy's grave. They sat quietly, feeling forlorn and heartbroken. Everyone found it hard to believe what had happened.

Benson the Boxer
felt so miserable.

He spent his days laying on the floor, hardly lifting his head.
He felt guilty for knocking the ball towards the road.
He felt guilty for not barking louder and he felt guilty for not running faster.

Benson's friends, Clara the kitten and Brigley the bear, came by to see Benson. They tried to bring him some comfort and to say how they missed Lucy too.

But Benson didn't feel like talking. He just wanted to be alone.

Benson's puppy friends held a remembrance dinner, in honour of Lucy. It was a special party to celebrate Lucy's life and the memories they shared. They brought hats and a cake. But Benson felt so miserable he didn't join in.

Clara tried to cheer Benson by giving him his very favourite dog bone, but the bone reminded him of sharing bones with Lucy and he imagined the accident happening all over again. Just thinking of the accident made his muscles tense, his breathing quicken, and he felt like he was going to be sick!

Benson was so miserable. He just wanted to hide. He no longer wanted to go outside. He no longer wanted to play.

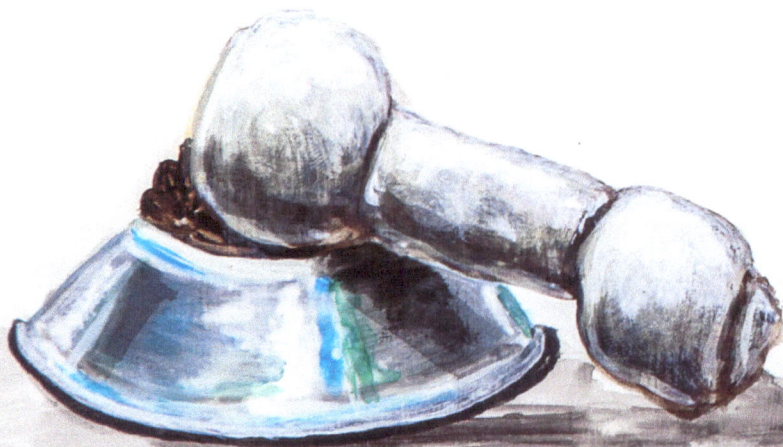

Benson always felt tired, but he couldn't sleep. He tossed and turned, wriggled, twisted, fidgeted and squirmed.

If Benson did finally fall asleep, his dreams were nightmares of the horrible day. He dreamt of running forever and ever, and ever... but never catching his friend Lucy.

Benson was now always frightened and anxious. Whenever he heard a truck go past, he would run and hide under the couch. The smallest of sounds would scare him. He almost jumped through the roof whenever there was a bang or a crash, a thud or a pop!

Benson was sure there was danger everywhere! He felt his world had been completely turned upside down.

Day after day Benson the Boxer sat by the door,
too afraid to go out and play,
too scared to leave the house,
too worried about cars and trucks,
too anxious to want to go to the park,
too upset to want to play with a bouncing ball,
too sad to want to do anything he used to enjoy.

Benson the Boxer
just felt miserable!

That is, until the day Uncle Boris came to visit.

Uncle Boris drove from his farm in his big, blue four-wheel-drive.

Benson loved Uncle Boris and he was glad to hear his voice, but he didn't rush out to greet him like he would normally do. Instead, Benson just peeked around the door and watched him with his big, sad, brown eyes.

Uncle Boris came inside. He sat in the big old leather armchair and quietly waited. He knew that Benson was very sad.

Slowly and softly Benson crept into the lounge room. He gently leapt up onto the chair opposite Uncle Boris. Somehow Benson knew that Uncle Boris would understand how he felt.

Uncle Boris looked over at Benson and gently said, "Benson, it is always sad when someone we love is no longer with us. This must be such a difficult time for you. I can see you are really hurting. Tell me about your friend Lucy."

Benson looked up at Lucy's photo that was sitting on the mantelpiece and began to tell Uncle Boris how Lucy had been his best friend ever since they were puppies. Benson started to cry, "It was my fault," he whimpered, "I was the one who knocked the ball onto the road."

Uncle Boris sat very still and listened…
Benson told him how he couldn't sleep, how his tummy
hurt and how he didn't want to play outside anymore.
He told Uncle Boris how he was scared to play with his
friends, because he was afraid something bad might
happen to them also.

When Benson finished speaking, Uncle Boris carefully explained how being frightened and anxious is quite normal when something bad, sad or scary happens to us.

Benson looked up and listened intently.
Uncle Boris told him that when something bad, sad or scary happens, our clever brain works very hard and very fast, taking action to protect us. It sends alert signals to our body to warn us of danger so that we can run fast, fight an enemy, or become very still and quiet.

"The brain's alert system is necessary," said Uncle Boris, "but problems can happen when the brain continues to remind us of how we were frightened, anxious or very sad – and it stays on alert, even after the terrible thing is no longer there, even when there is nothing to be scared of."

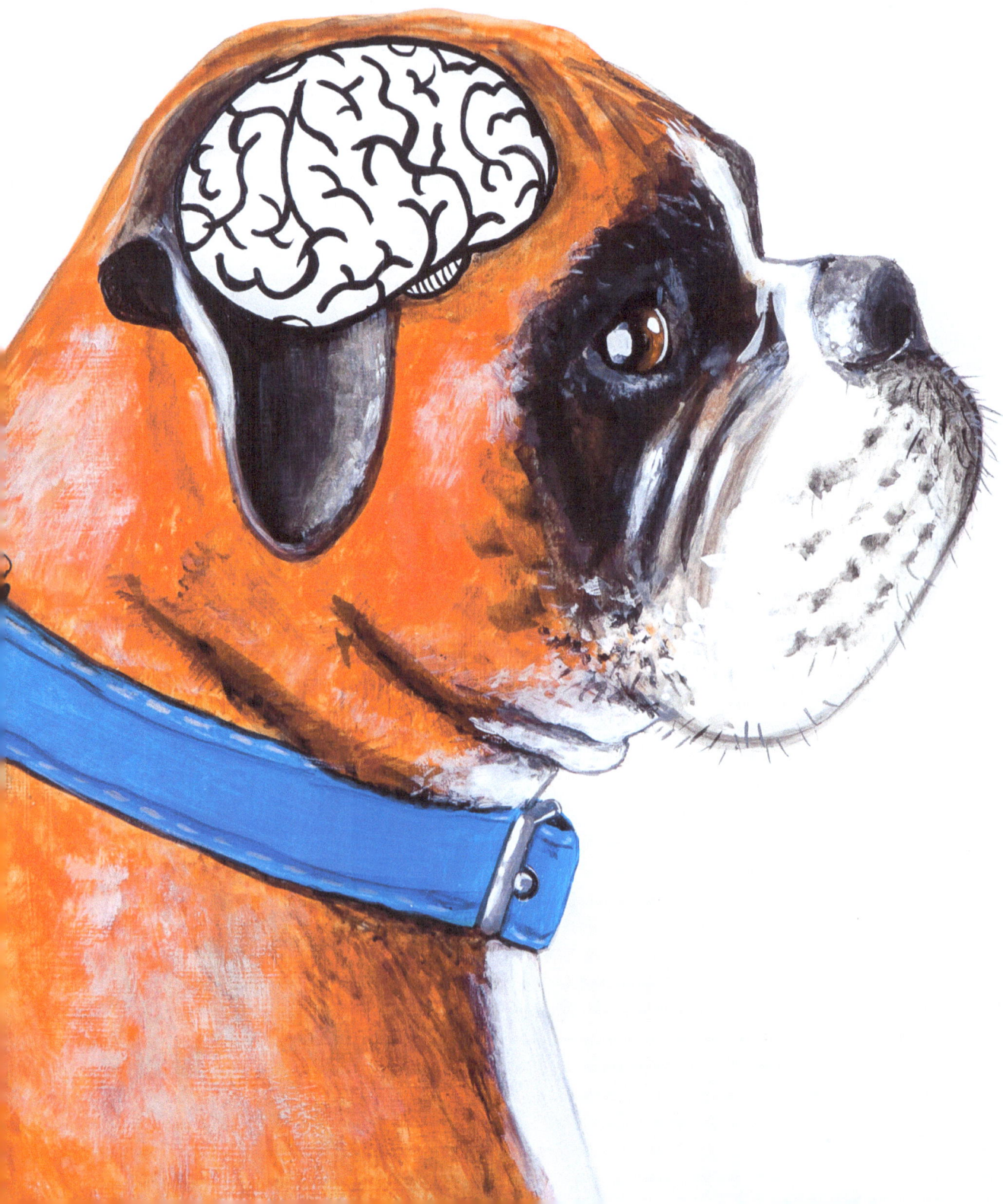

We might hear a sound, see a sight, sniff a smell, eat a treat or maybe touch a memory.

We often recognise something that reminds us of the bad, sad or scary time and we can become terrified all over again…
    and again…
        and again...

We continue to be unable to think clearly, we get mud-dled and confused, and we stay feeling miserable - even when there is no danger at all.

Benson began to understand. He remembered the day of the accident, the noise of the truck and the honk of the cars. Once again he felt a cold shiver of fear. He remembered the bounce of the ball and the screech of brakes. His terrified heart thumped and pounded inside his puppy chest. He remembered the smell of the grass, and his head began to ache and spin all over again.

Benson knew there were so many things that now frightened him. He had stopped doing what he used to enjoy. He spent his days hiding under chairs, slinking behind curtains, burying himself under blankets and sitting alone inside cupboards.

Benson didn't go out or do things anymore because he wanted to feel safe. But Benson was trapped.

It was like sitting in a box all day! Doing nothing, going nowhere…but still feeling miserable!

"Benson," said Uncle Boris kindly, "Lucy was a very close friend, and you saw something very terrible happen to her. This sad, bad and scary time has remained part of your memory."

"After a terrible experience, it is hard to get back to doing things we used to enjoy," Uncle Boris explained. "We can feel that we don't have the energy to do anything anymore. It's hard to get up, get out and get going again. Getting well takes time."

Benson slunk off his chair and onto the floor. He began to scratch his back on the carpet. He knew that Uncle Boris could help him, but he felt nervous and very uncomfortable.

Uncle Boris lay down on the floor to reassure Benson.
He said, "Benson, I am here to help you to begin to be
well again, step by step, little by little. I want to help
you not to feel miserable anymore." He placed a caring
paw under Benson's chin.

"Benson," Uncle Boris said, "You may not feel it at the moment, but in the past you have been a very brave and   courageous dog."

"Do you remember the time you were lost in the bush?"
Benson nodded. He remembered the five nights he was lost and all alone. He also remembered how he had found food, slept under logs, followed streams and made it back home. Yes – he had been brave and he had survived!

Uncle Boris also reminded Benson how he had bravely fought off angry Alex the Alsatian and all his bully friends, at the beach last summer. Benson gave a little smile as he remembered the way he had done a terrific Tae Kwon Do kick, giving the four bullies such a surprise that they quickly turned and ran away. Yes, he thought – I have been courageous and strong.

Uncle Boris gently said, "Benson, I know you are really struggling at the moment, would you like things to be a little bit better?"

Benson nodded. He thought about the fun times he used to enjoy with his friends.

He thought about playing, and exploring, running and hiding. But mostly he remembered how he used to laugh! How he would roll onto his back and laugh – just at the fun of life! Finally he said, "I want to be able to do the things I used to do. I want to have fun again."

"You can," encouraged Uncle Boris, "Together we can help you through this. Where would you like to start?

Benson stood at the window
and paused...

He stood thinking, remembering and looking outside…
He knew he would never forget his friend Lucy. She
would always hold a special place in his heart.

After standing at the window for quite some time, Benson finally said, "You know Uncle Boris, I think I'd like to go outside again."

Uncle Boris gave a warm, reassuring smile, "Good for you, Benson," he said, "I'll come with you. Let's go."

Author: Karen J Ferry

Karen is in private practice as a Neuropsychotherapist. She holds degrees in Education, a Master's Degree in Counselling (University of Queensland) and is a certified Clinical Neuropsychotherapy Practitioner. Karen has also been an educator for over 35 years and has experience in primary and secondary classrooms, and has worked with families in home education environments. She now specializes in counselling students who have suffered situations of loss, and those facing difficulties at home or school, offering neuropsychotherapy strategies to nurture, empower and move a child forward from difficult or traumatic situations.

www.brainsmarteducation.com

Illustrator: Selinah Bull

Australian artist Selinah Bull creates original works that span multiple media. From personal artworks to fine art photography, each piece is created with love and attention to detail. Selinah has loved art and design for as long as she can remember and she especially enjoys creating fun, imaginative and whimsical paintings for children. Her inspiration comes from being able to touch people's lives with her artworks. Selinah lives and works on the Far North Coast of NSW, Australia.

www.selinahbull.com

Additional Resources:

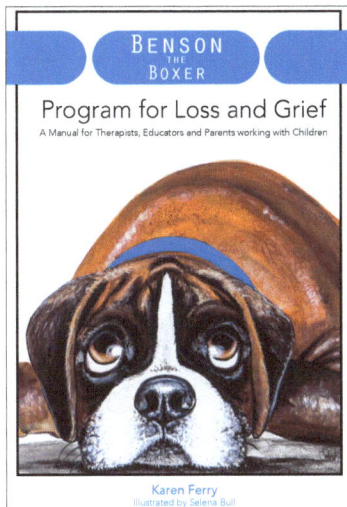

Benson the Boxer storybook is accompanied by a **manual**. The content of the manual is based on neuroscience research, explaining how the brain is affected by grief, loss and trauma. The manual holds guidelines for the effective use of the storybook, Benson the Boxer, and will assist the user with neuroscience explanations, discussion starters and therapy based activities for young clients and students.

Client work books are also available. The workbooks are designed to maximise a young person's understanding and learning experience by completing activities that are colourful, readable, interesting and activity based. The workbooks are a fun, non-confrontational tool designed to assist in generating discussion and provide activity based opportunities for young people to explore emotional reactions and behaviours associated with situations of trauma, loss and grief.

JUNIOR WORKBOOK

SENIOR WORKBOOK

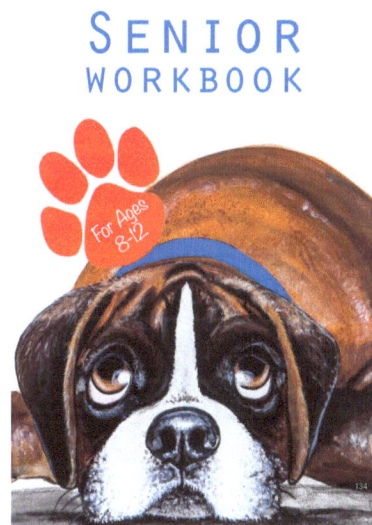

Workbook 1: The Junior level workbook is designed to assist children in the 4-7 age group.

Workbook 2: The Senior level workbook is designed to assist children in the 8-12 age group.

Please Note: Due to the variability in children's cognitive abilities and emotional understanding, these age groups are only to be used as a guide.

Note: The Junior and Senior Workbooks are contained within the Manual.

www.ingramcontent.com/pod-product-compliance
Lightning Source LLC
Chambersburg PA
CBHW060815270326
41930CB00002B/50